Bride of the War
My Journey from Liverpool to Chicago

(Title inspired by my granddaughter Lauren at age 15.)

By
Doris Alma (Taylor) Provenzano

Copyright © 2018

Publisher: ECS Executive Career Services & DeskTop Publishing, Inc.
Steven Provenzano, Editor

Ebook ISBN: 978-0-9633558-4-3
Print Book ISBN: 978-19767545-3-1

CHAPTER ONE

The city of Liverpool sits on the river Mersey in northern England and was once one of the busiest shipping ports in the world. Slaves were brought in from Africa and sold at the docks there over 200 years ago, and there are still chains attached to the walls; a sad reminder of man's inhumanity to man. Many of the slaves were sent to America to pick cotton, which was then sent back to Liverpool for processing in the cotton mills. Ships returned to America, delivering guns and cannons. It's home to many Irish immigrants from across the Irish Sea, just a three-hour ferryboat ride away. It was also a stopping off place for many immigrants from Europe on their way to America; they went there to find work in the many factories, iron foundries and the Lancashire cotton mills, hoping to make enough money to finish their journey. Many of them got no further, having families to support, that's why Liverpool is a melting pot, the same as America; in fact, it was often called "Little America."

Long before anyone ever heard of the Beatles and eleven years before World War II started, I was born in a Liverpool suburb called Fazakerley. Growing up with two brothers and a sister, we would play outside until it was dark, which was ten o'clock at night in the summer. We would play a game called rounders; it is much like American baseball but with four bases, then home. We used four trees in the street for bases.

Wintertime was just the opposite; it was dark at four o'clock, short days and long nights. We spent many nights around our small fire in the living room. My Dad would tell us stories about his seven years in India, how he rode a horse as a member of the Queen's Cavalry, and how they all suffered from the heat. It would be as high as 120 degrees, and they were used to cool, mild, English weather. He was supposed to stay two years, but the army kept him there for seven. He joined the army when he was 17.

My dad had a very harsh childhood and a very strict Victorian upbringing with a hard mother. He had three brothers and a sister, who all left, or where told to leave, when they reached their teens. His brother Winston left at 14, ran away to Canada and worked as a lumber jack, he came home at age 28, knocked on the door, his mother opened it and then slammed it in his face. His brother Joe went off to London to seek his fortune, brother Harry got married and left, and his sister, my Auntie Lu, ran off to London and joined the chorus on stage.

He said when they were little, they all sat on a bench in the kitchen while their parents ate their meals. When they were through, they would get up, leave the table and the kids would sit down and eat what was left. He never went back after the war, he married my mum and I never saw his. He would meet his Dad at the Liverpool football ground, watch the game and say goodbye. My mum said his Dad was a good man, but completely under his wife's thumb, probably a case of peace at any price.

My mum's family where the exact opposite, she was one of ten children, five boys and five girls, a big loving family. My Grandma Christopher was left to raise them on her own, while my Grandpa was away fighting, in World War I, from 1914 to 1918. She was little, barely five feet tall, but she had a heart of gold. I was her first grandchild, and we were very close. I would visit her on a Saturday, and help out, or go to the store for her, along with her dog, a German Shepherd, named Dixie. As a rare treat, she would take me to the local cinema to see the latest Shirley Temple movie. We had some great days out on south road beach, a stretch of sand off the river Mersey, we would pack salmon sandwiches and hopefully eat them before someone would run past and kick sand into them. We took gallons of lemonade, and bought pots of tea from the vendors; if we had any money left we could buy an ice cream, a luxury at the time.

We depended on the fireplace for everything, it had an oven connected to it, my mother cooked and baked in it. There were no dials or temperature gages, but everything came out perfect. We made our toast on it using a long fork. We boiled the kettle on it to make our tea, and heated the iron on it to iron our clothes. That was quite a project, first we would have to clean the soot off, then attach a metal shield to cover it, by then it was cooled down and we had to start all over again.

Our upstairs bedrooms were cold. All we had throughout the house was the fire in the living room, no central heating. My sister Margie and I would take the oven shelf out, wrap it in newspaper and put it in the bed to warm our feet. It was hard getting out of that bed in the morning, we went down the stairs real fast, to get in front of the fire, my dear little mum would have it going for us. She called that fire the heart of our home; I didn't think so when I had to clean out the ashes.

The fire's most useful function was to dry our clothes; the English weather is so wet and rainy. On wash day the clothes would go into a boiler with a gas jet under it. She would stir the clothes around with a wooden stick, lift them out with the stick, and drop them into cold water in the bathtub next to it. She'd rinse them out by hand, then put them through the mangle, between the rollers. All by hand, my mum would get everything washed, wrung through the mangle, hang them out on the line, then the rain would come down. Everything was brought back in the house and hung around the fire on a clothes rack called a maiden; never ending work for my mum.

I had chronic Bronchitis all of my life. My mum would put a kettle on the fire, sit me in front of it with a sheet over my head, and I would inhale the steam, there were no antibiotics in those days, we had to do the best we could.

When I was ten years old, my baby brother Billy was born. I was so excited when my mum brought him home, and since I was the oldest I could hold him on my lap. I tried to make him look at me but he just kept staring at the light in the ceiling. We found out weeks later that he was blind, and that flashes of light was all he could see. My mum offered to donate one of her eyes, but was told there was nothing to attach it to. He went on to have a full life and lost no time in learning to read and write Braille.

A big event every year was the running of the Grand National race on the course near our house; we would sneak in and sit on top of the railway embankment and watch the horses go over the jumps. It was a long and grueling race for them. One year we saw a horse fall, and the Bobby [policeman] hit it between the eyes with his club to put it out of its misery, it was very traumatic for us kids.

My mum had a great sense of humor; she could keep us going with her cheerful manner. When she made a bowl of Jell-O for us, a rare treat, she said "just put it at the foot of our bed, it will soon set". We never had a refrigerator, our food was bought fresh daily; my mum would walk to the shops every day, and one bottle of milk was delivered every morning. I would sneak out early and eat the cream off the top of the bottle where it settled and then put the top back on.

We all walked everywhere; the only person I knew with a car was our family doctor. I did ride in it once, he came to the house when I had diphtheria, and he rolled me inside a big red blanket and put me in the back seat, and took me to the hospital when I was seven years old. My mum said I almost died that time, their were no antibiotics in those days. Margie, Bobby and I had just about every disease a kid could get. Mumps, Measles, Chicken Pox, Scarlet fever, the only inoculations available were for Small Pox.

The 1930s were very hard years for a family to survive; their was a depression and men couldn't find work. After the boom of the roaring twenties, following World War I, the whole country was in a slump. When our shoes wore out we would put cardboard inside to cover the hole in the sole, until my dad could get a piece of leather to repair them. He also cut our hair, mine was chopped real short just like the boy's; I hated it but I had no choice. And we mended our clothes. Luckily we wore a uniform to school, a white blouse and navy blue jumper, and we wore it every day with long black knit stockings.

My Grandma had a neighbour with a daughter, an only child, who gave her hand-me-downs to me, so I had some nice things. I remember one pretty dress, it was Salmon Pink, I felt like a movie star when I wore it, she also gave me a Grey flannel suit with a pleated skirt. When my mum was in the hospital having my brother Billy, I was looking for it, to wear it to Sunday school. I almost cried when I found it, my Dad had put the pleated skirt under the sofa cushion to press it, it was a wrinkled mess, I suppose he meant well.

CHAPTER TWO

My whole life changed when World War II started in 1939. Food and clothes where rationed and my mother worked miracles with what she could get. My dad planted a vegetable garden; the potatoes were a lifesaver some days. Once in a while a rumor would start that something off ration, such as fruit was available and my mum would dash out and stand in the never-ending lines.

It wasn't too much longer before the air raids started. The planes were aiming for the ships in the port of Liverpool, and the docks were hit hard. Of course England is an Island, so we depended on ships for everything. Much of our food ended up in the river Mersey; a whole ship loaded with sugar was hit and all of the sugar ended up in the river, my mum said they had been waiting weeks for that sugar. Most of the boats never even made it to Liverpool; German U. boats sank them in the Atlantic.

As the air raids became more frequent, we were given an Anderson air raid shelter. It came in sections and had to be bolted together, the sides were six feet tall and the top rounded, it was made of corrugated steel. My dad and brother dug a hole three feet down and six feet square and stood the shelter in it. The three feet that stuck up over the hole was covered with dirt and sod that also helped to disguise it and cover the shiny surface, as we were in a strict blackout. All of the house windows were covered with heavy blackout curtains to block the light, as the planes would circle overhead looking for targets. It was so dark that when I walked home at night, I'd run my hand along the fence, until I hit the gatepost I knew I was home. My aunt said she bumped into something in the blackout and asked, "are you alive or are you a lamp post?" A voice replied, "I am a lamp post," -- she ran all the way home.

When the raids started to come every night, my dad decided to build bunk beds in the shelter so we could sleep in it when the sirens rang out. We had been roused out of bed and led down the stairs by my mother, into the cold night air and into the damp shelter, with only a dirt floor. Now we were tucked in blankets and given a flashlight and comic books to keep us quiet. My dad never got out of his warm bed. He said, "Hitler isn't going to give me pneumonia, and besides if the house gets hit, you will have two stories worth of bricks on top of you!" This of course was a great source of comfort to my mother. Most of the damage in our neighborhood was caused by incendiary bombs; they would stick in the roofs of houses and burn. Easy for the home guard to put out if they landed on the ground, but difficult if it was on the roof. The land mines were the worst; they would float down on a parachute and drift along the ground destroying everything in their path.

We tried to keep to a normal schedule with our schooling until the day raids started; a school in Liverpool was hit, and all the children were killed. Our teachers split the classes up into small groups and we were sent to the homes of volunteers who had a room to spare. They came to each house and gave us our lessons and homework, so we wouldn't all be in one place during the raids.

Our next big worry was that the enemy would use gas. All of us children where issued gas masks and told to carry them everywhere. We thought we where pretty cool and put them in a shoulder bag. Mine was black patent leather. One day a mobile unit came to our school and we were all ordered to go inside while they turned the gas on to check for leaks, not deadly gas of course.

My friends and I were not old enough to worry about survival the way the grown-ups did; we made a game out of searching for pieces of shrapnel the day after an air raid. We would be quite pleased to find some with German markings. Mostly imprints of swastikas, I saved mine in a shoebox.

The only time I was really scared and worried was one day after a big raid. I was sent to grandma's house to help her clean, as I had always done on a Saturday morning. When I got off the streetcar at my usual stop, I didn't recognize anything. The area had been bombed, there was glass and food all over the road from the shops nearby. The police were patrolling the area to prevent looting. There was a huge crater where the Windsor Castle Pub had stood. We heard later that the owner of the pub had gone back in, after the air raid warning had sounded, to get the money out of the safe. He never made it back out, as the building got a direct hit. That pub had been my landmark. I walked up the hill toward my grandma's house, afraid to turn the corner in case her house was gone. My grandma was fine, but the street next to hers was flattened, she was home alone because my grandpa was out with the bomb disposal group. They were sent out after a raid to put out fires caused by incendiary bombs, and to detonate any unexploded bombs. His age group was too old for the army, but they were needed in the home guard.

Some nights before a raid, the planes would circle overhead and drop flares to light up the area. The British anti-aircraft guns would try to shoot them down with tracer bullets; we called them flaming onions. It was like fireworks and we wanted to watch; we were constantly being told to get back inside the shelter. We had an old anti-aircraft gun that was wheeled around the neighborhood, we found out after the war that it was useless. What it did do was rattle our windows; luckily we had criss-cross tape on the glass so it wouldn't shatter. One night they did catch a man signaling the planes, at the aircraft plant near our house. It was a factory that built the Spitfire airplanes, that was why we had so many raids around us, even though we lived in the suburbs. The bombers also aimed for the shipping at the Liverpool docks.

I was so glad I lived in the suburbs, because it was decided that children would have to be evacuated out of the cities. The first plan was to send them all on ships to Australia, America and Canada, but that was stopped when the U-boats sank them in the Atlantic Ocean. All those children where lost at sea. After that, they were all put on trains and sent to the countryside, to stay with strange families. It was sad to see them on the newsreels, with their nametags and their little suitcases saying tearful goodbyes to their mothers. Some of them never saw their families again for five years, or never, if their families where killed in the raids.

England was not prepared for war - every scrap of metal that could be salvaged was rounded up. The iron railings, fences and gates around the parks were torn down to be used for munitions. Nothing went to waste; the whole country was geared up to survive. My father said thank God for the English Channel! At least we had that between us and France, and the enemy couldn't just walk over to England.

CHAPTER THREE

In 1943 the American troops started landing in Liverpool, we didn't know it at the time, but they where preparing for the invasion of Europe. A camp was set up on the Aintree racecourse where I had watched the Grand National race as a child. The King and Queen and Princess Elizabeth and Princess Margaret drove past on their way to the Royal box, all of us children lined up along the street and waved our little union jack flags. We where thrilled when the princesses hung out of the back of the limousine and waved to us.

Another camp was set up about ten minutes from my house in Kirby. The American soldiers filled a void for all of us young girls, as all of the British boys were away fighting. The British soldiers were fighting in Italy and Burma, and my uncle Jim was with General Montgomery's troops fighting in the desert. They were called the Desert Rats, and he was in the tank corps. He and three more of my uncles, my mum's brothers, were all in the army. We were invited to the camp dances since the GIs couldn't dance with each other.

One night I met a shy 19-year old named Tony, and we began going out to movies; after a few dates, he asked if he could meet my family. I had discouraged it, because my father had forbidden me to go near any soldiers; I was 16 at the time. Of course, being a teenager I didn't listen. One night on the way home, we were about to board the streetcar, when I saw my mum and Dad ahead of me. I tried to duck back but my Dad saw me and said, "you, get on this streetcar, right now". We rode to the end of the line, where I would walk home and Tony and any other G.I.s would ride an army truck back to the camp.

As we got off, my Dad said, "all of you, back to the house." I was scared and told Tony to go, and I would face the music alone; he said, "no, I'm going with you," so Tony, his friend and my friend all walked back to the house with me. My mum and dad went in first, my dad opened the door and I introduced everyone. Tony put his hand out and said, "pleased to meet you sir", my dad was very impressed, not only was Tony polite but he was very smart, uniform pressed, buttons polished, shoes shined. My poor little mum was a nervous wreck, busily making tea in the kitchen, waiting for the fireworks to start, we all sat down and had a short visit, and Tony and his friend had to get back to camp. After that, Tony was a frequent visitor to our house.

When the commanding officer was told that soldiers were invited for dinner at a local home, the guys were told they could bring food since our rations didn't go very far. One day, Tony pulled up in front of our house, stopped too quickly and ended up with a dozen broken eggs on the back seat of the jeep. That was the first time I saw my mother almost cry; we where only allowed one egg a week on our ration books. Another time my mum managed to get a roast from the local butcher; she babied it all afternoon in the fire oven; we all waited in great anticipation. When she sliced it, there was a fist-sized lump of fat in the middle, then we all almost cried. That had used up six ration books, and to think that it had made it through the U-boats from Argentina. Tony also brought a turkey for my mum to cook; my dad and brother ate so much they were sick, they were not used to eating so much meat.

My brother Bobby who was 14 and sister Margie who was 12 got along great with Tony. He was like part of the family; he and his friends would kid with them that if the Barrage Balloons where cut loose, England would sink into ocean. They were huge, inflated silver balloons that had cables hanging down, designed to snag enemy planes that tried to get through, they worked pretty good during the air raids.

We had a great New Year's Eve party at my Grandma's house, Tony and some of his friends came, my uncle Harold played the piano, and we all had a sing-song.

CHAPTER FOUR

D-Day, June 1944, the biggest invasion in the history of the world took place.

Tony's company was in charge of getting men and supplies over the English channel to France. We had to say goodbye, and I thought I'd never see him again, even after he said he would come back and marry me.

Tony was in the medical corps, and ended up being stationed in a hospital in LeHavre, France. He wrote many letters to me, saying he would make it back to Liverpool after the war. I wrote back and said I would be there. He said if he did, we would get married. Tony started the paper work, and completed all of the army red tape, plus papers filled out by his family in the States. I had to fill out papers on my end, and also show I had my parent's permission to go ahead. Tony's commanding officer sent a representative to my house to interview my parents since I was under age. I was seventeen and a half. All the papers where officially signed and everything approved, then all we had to do was wait for the war to end.

V.E. Day, Victory in Europe day, finally came in May 1945. I was working in a theater downtown and when I walked outside it was total pandemonium, people where dancing in the streets, it was such a relief to know that five years of war were finally over. Meanwhile Tony's outfit had been taking care of released American prisoners of war. They had to be patched up and made ready for the long trip home. He was kept over in France for the rest of the year with his company. The war in the Pacific was still raging, Japan would not surrender, and the plan was to send them all over to the Pacific to fight. President Harry Truman decided to drop the Atomic bomb on Hiroshima, then when that didn't end it, another was dropped on Nagasaki. They finally surrendered in September 1945.

It took three more months before Tony could get across the channel to England. I knew he was trying to make it but I didn't know when I would see him. On the 10th of December 1945, I was standing in line at the local cinema with a group of friends, when I felt a tap on my shoulder. I turned around and there he was, it was hard to believe it was actually him, what a surprise. His first words were, "come on we are getting married."

My Mum worked miracles getting it all together. We made arrangements with the priest, then my next problem was finding a dress; clothes were still rationed. Our butcher's daughter had just been married, and she said I could borrow her dress. It was white satin and had a veil. It was a little short for me as she was shorter, but it fit O.K. My sister and my friend also borrowed dresses.

We hired a Rolls Royce Limousine and rode in style to the church. I had managed to get a beautiful bouquet of white pom-pom mums; my aunt gave me a white prayer book and a silver cardboard horseshoe for good luck. My mum managed to get a small family party together. That was our wedding day, December 21st. 1945.

We had a three-day honeymoon in a resort called Blackpool on the Lancashire coast. Miserable English weather, cold, lashing down rain, but we didn't care, we where together and in love.

We got back home on Christmas Eve, hung up our stockings, and Santa put a pair of slippers and some hard to get candy in them, bless my little mum. Tony had requested a two-week extension on his leave since he was now married, but it had not come through. He said he was not about to leave on Christmas day, so he stayed over until Boxing day the 26th. That is a big English holiday. It dates back to when the rich people had their Christmas on the 25th, then the poor would get the leftover food on the 26th. Whatever gifts had been re-wrapped and boxed, that the rich people didn't want, that became their Christmas. When he got back to France, expecting to be arrested for being AWOL he was told the extension had been sent. It arrived at our house on the 27th, delayed because of the holiday. There was no way he could make it back to England.

The one disappointing thing on our wedding day was that the photographer never showed up; we have no pictures of our wedding. I went downtown after Tony left and complained. They said they were sorry, that everything was still a mess around there from all the bomb damage. They offered to take me on my own, so I got dressed up again. Of course my flowers where all dead, so I posed with my silver cardboard horseshoe and my small white prayer book, I still have that photograph.

CHAPTER FIVE

In February 1946, Tony and his company got their orders to pack up and get ready to go home, they were all loaded onto troop ships for their voyage back to the states. I got my orders from the army to stay put, until they figured out what to do with us. He left LeHavre not knowing what was going to happen next. There were 100,000 G.I. Brides to be transported over the ocean, from England and Europe.

In March I got my orders to report to Tidworth on the south coast of England, where we would be made ready for our journey to America. First I was told to have a complete physical by my family doctor. My mum took me and we filled out the required paperwork. My orders were to leave on April 24th. I packed my case and boarded a train in Liverpool at Lime St. Station. My mum and auntie Connie saw me off. I had said goodbye to my Dad and sister and brothers at the house and felt quite cheerful and excited, until the train started to move. I looked back and saw my mum collapse on my aunt's shoulder; it finally dawned on me what a huge step this was. I cried all the way to London, along with some of the other girls who came from my area. We changed trains at Waterloo station and took the one to Tidworth. It turned out to be an old army camp, and had been used by British soldiers. We were put into barracks, assigned a cot to sleep in, given a mess kit and lined up for our food, army style.

We were waited on by German prisoners who, to say the least, were not too thrilled to be waiting on a group of women. They still had their uniforms on, a bit tattered but proud, just like the ones I had seen cleaning up the bomb damage in downtown Liverpool.

Before I left Liverpool, my mum had collected the clothing coupons from the whole family, and we went shopping. She said "you are not landing in America and meeting Tony's family looking like a refugee." I bought a beautiful blue wool suit, and a white crepe blouse, as well as new shoes and some needed accessories, never thinking until later how selfish that was.

We were treated like soldiers with a bed check every night; they came around with a flashlight, counting us in our cots. One of the girls got so homesick she climbed out of the window and went home. We put a pillow under her blanket so she wasn't missed before it was too late. Quite a ceremony was made out of taking our ration books away from us, dropping them in a trashcan and saying "you won't need these in America."

A few days after we arrived, we were told to strip down and were given army robes to wear. They had belonged to the women's army group that had been stationed there. We were all lined up in a long corridor, and as we got to the front of the line we were taken into a room, one by one. An army doctor and a nurse checked me over from head to toe. I told them I had a complete physical before I left home, and I had the papers to prove it. They told me it was ordered by the government, they wanted to make sure none of us where bringing diseases into the country.

While we were standing in that line, not knowing what was going to happen next, I became very nervous. We had been seeing horrible pictures of the concentration camps in Germany on the front page of the newspapers as they were being liberated. The girl at the front of the line would disappear into the room, the door would close and we didn't see her come out. It sounds silly now, but the newspaper pictures were of women standing in line naked, waiting for what they thought were showers, and they were gas chambers. Our group was obviously going out of a different door, to get dressed.

We were told they were trying to get ships lined up to take us all to the states, but there were so many of us. Liberty ships were brought over to take some girls, and I ended up on one. I just missed getting on the Queen Mary, the largest ship in the world. It had been used as a troop ship during the war, and it carried thousands of girls and hundreds of babies. Our ship, the President Tyler, had about five hundred girls and one hundred babies. It took us ten days to cross the Atlantic. The Queen Mary passed us going back to England, that only took five days.

It was a rough voyage. Our ship with small, open sides was tossed around in the Atlantic ocean like a toy. One of the girls was so sea sick that I took care of her baby. In between, we played endless games of Five Hundred Rummy, and tried to make the best of it. Before the ship had left the port at Southampton, some of the girls got a phone call on the ship to shore phone, from their parents; that's all they needed, they got off and went home. While we were boarding the ship we saw a boat load of British soldiers coming in from Europe, many of them wounded and on crutches, it was the first British soldiers I had seen. One of them shouted out to us, we are home girls you don't have to leave. We didn't pay much attention; we were on our way to America and our new lives with our husbands.

CHAPTER SIX

We finally caught sight of land, and what a sight it was. The whole New York skyline, right before our eyes. We were thrilled to pass the statue of liberty in the harbor, but puzzled about the green and yellow flashes racing along the pier and bridges; we found out later they were New York taxicabs. All of the tug boats in the harbour came out to meet us, blasting their horns, as they had been doing for the returning G.I.s, to welcome them home. Our Captain got on the bullhorn and asked them to keep it down as all the babies were sleeping. We were looking forward to getting off that boat and we were very disappointed when they told us we had to stay on board, as a train strike was about to start.

We were kept on the boat for several days, when one of the officials kindly rounded us up and said, "I am going to give you a sight seeing trip of New York." We were put on a bus and driven around the city. It was mind boggling to see all the lights after coming from a blackout, and it was the first time any of us had seen skyscrapers. I had a stiff neck from looking up through the bus window. Then it was back on the boat, to await our fate.

Our husbands had been given orders to stay in their home in their own states and told that if they came to New York, they wouldn't guarantee that they would be able to get back home, because of the train strike. Tony was living with his family in St. Louis, Missouri, and was promised that the army would get me there.

After another day of waiting, the Captain told us the strike had been called off, so off we went onto the buses and straight to Grand Central Station to board the train. I was sitting on the steps of the train holding the baby I had been helping to care for on the boat, when a reporter from a New York newspaper took my picture. Apparently, a G.I. bride boat from Belgium had docked before us and a baby had died, there were no provisions made for taking care of babies, strange water and no formula. We were very lucky on our ship, because we had a Doctor and nurses coming home from France, and they took good care of us and the babies.

The reporter was looking for a story, and my picture appeared in the paper the next day with the caption, POOR TIRED G.I. BRIDE WITH HER SICK BABY. It wasn't even my baby. We were in the station quite a while waiting to board the train, when one of the porters told us "Sorry ladies the strike is on." Luckily the American Red Cross came to the rescue, with sandwiches and cartons of milk for us and milk for the babies. One of the porters, who must have felt sorry for such a sad looking bunch, stayed behind and pulled down the Pullman beds, so we could go to sleep on the train.

CHAPTER SEVEN

We all settled down in our beds, not knowing what tomorrow would bring, then during the night we felt the train move, an army transport was pushing us along the tracks. We were pushed all the way to a town called Rome, New York. As we pulled into the station we were told to get ready to get off. When we did, we saw cars and taxis lined up outside. Apparently the townspeople had been told of our plight and had volunteered their vehicles to transport us to a nearby air base. As we walked into the station I heard my first American juke box playing Prisoner of Love, by Perry Como, and a little boy shouting, "wow, look at all the taxis," for the first time, I really felt like I was in America.

We were driven to the base located out of town, put up in the barracks, and told that they were waiting for permission to fly us to our different states. Meanwhile we were treated very well, seated in the dining room and given our first real meal in days. While we were eating, I was paged over the loud speaker, the Red cross had tracked me down, and Tony was on the long distance phone. The first thing he asked was, "Where are you?" When I said I was in Rome, he said, "What are you doing in Italy?." I explained what had happened, and that they were trying to get permission to fly me to St. Louis. He was surprised but relieved to hear that I was safe.

On the second day, one of the officers took us shopping. I bought my first pair of American white sandals; all we had were our heavy leather British shoes, and it was really hot. By now it was almost June, and we were not used to the heat. We were asked to name the one food we would like that we hadn't seen all during the war.

I said we had not had a banana in years. There I was, again, in the next day's newspaper, a picture of one of the officers with a big bunch of bananas, with the caption, BANANAS FOR BRIDES, from then on; I learned to keep quiet.

Permission finally came through to fly us to our destinations, then on the same day, the train strike ended. We packed up again and were driven back to the station, to once again board the trains. I had befriended a girl name Kathleen who was going to Kentucky, we where both excited about finally seeing our husbands, and decided to get our best clothes out and try to be ready before the train pulled into the station in St. Louis, where we had to say goodbye. When we did arrive I was surprised to see Tony standing there in shorts looking very sun tanned, I had only ever seen him in a uniform, and I hadn't seen him for six months. His mum, dad, sister and brothers were with him; there were hugs all around, then we stepped outside the station and the heat hit me. I had never felt anything like it before; it was 100 degrees and very humid. We rode to the house and when we got there, the first thing I did was take that blue wool suit off, that I had saved for that day. I put it in a box and told Tony to mail it to my sister in England, there was no way I could wear it in America. Tony's family had fixed up a room in their house for us because there was a big housing shortage. All the servicemen were coming home, and nothing had been built during the war; everything had been focused on war material and planes, tanks and the like.

The biggest surprise for me was to find Tony's family speaking Italian, although his sister and brothers spoke English and his mother tried for my sake. It was quite an adjustment for me. At least I had met one of them before, his brother Santo, had been stationed in England with the Seabees, and had made it from the south of England by train to Liverpool, to visit Tony. He came to my house and met my family, that helped a little, at least I knew one member. Tony's other brothers where Joe, age 18, and the youngest one Louie, who was only eleven. He fascinated me because he would speak perfect Italian to his parents, then turn to me and speak perfect English, without missing a beat. His sister, the only girl, was 14, named Nimfa, a very unusual name, named after her Italian grandmother.

Sicily in Red   *Sicilian Flag*

Both of Tony's parents came to America with their families from Sicily in the 20's and settled in an Italian neighborhood in Chicago. They met and were married in Chicago and had five children, Tony being the first-born. When Tony was ten years old they all went back to Burgio Sicily for a visit, because his mum was homesick. They stayed for one year and Louie was born there; his Dad had a house built for the family, and it's still there.

They came back to America because Mussolini was starting to round up all the young boys to train them for the coming war, the way Hitler was doing in Germany with the Hitler Youth movement. Tony and Santo were just at the right age, so it was decided it was time to get out of the country. They came back and settled in St. Louis near relatives, then his dad developed a heart problem and couldn't work any more. Tony had to go to work to help out, being the oldest. He delivered newspapers and worked in a shoe repair shop, and never had a chance to go to high school. He worked to help the family until he was drafted into the army, and sent to England where I met him.

We only lived in St. Louis three months, which was enough. Between the heat and the whole town going wild over baseball (the St. Louis Cardinals were in a race for the championship), it was all foreign to me. I would try and stay outside as it was hot in the house, then I would get sunburned; it was too hot. Tony took me to the local cinema to cool off; it was the only place with air conditioning. The iceman would come to the house carrying big blocks of ice on his shoulder, and he would put it in an old wooden icebox, it had a drip pan underneath it, to catch the water as it was melting.

There were watermelon stands set up along some of the streets, and I was fascinated watching the people eating this strange looking fruit. Tony persuaded me to try it, and I was so disappointed when I did, it was such a beautiful strawberry colour, but it tasted flat and watery, I had expected it to taste more fruity, and it had so many seeds.

CHAPTER EIGHT

In August the family decided to move to Chicago. Tony wasn't feeling well and losing weight, and no one could find work; his dad thought they would be better off back in the old neighborhood, near old friends and relatives. We didn't have a car, so we all rode a Greyhound bus to Chicago; Tony had bought a bedroom set, and we sent that ahead of us with the movers. We moved into a three-bedroom apartment on the third floor of a building in the old Italian neighborhood in the city, with his family. In those days, all of the different ethnic groups stayed together in their own part of the city. As each new batch of immigrants came over they settled with their own countrymen, bound together by language. I made my first American friends: the two girls next door, around my age, and Tony's cousins. They took me downtown on the bus to show me the city, I could not get over all the bright lights, and State street was like a fairyland.

The first thing Tony's father did was get me a job in a factory, a short walk away. I had never worked in a factory before, and I hated it, but the people were very nice, and we all had to work. His father couldn't work and Tony was still losing weight, not feeling well and didn't have a job. One day I came home from work and Tony was gone, his father said he had taken him to the doctor, and he said he thought Tony had tuberculosis. He was admitted into Hines Veteran's hospital, in Maywood Illinois. That was quite a shock for me, I didn't get to see him go. Maywood is a suburb of Chicago, a one-hour train ride from the city. I was only able to visit him on the weekends; the whole family would visit him on Sunday. I wanted to move near the hospital but his father wouldn't let me. He said he was responsible for me, and I shouldn't be living on my own. The old Italians were very protective of their daughters; Tony's sister couldn't go out, anywhere, alone. I did not appreciate this at the time, and was very resentful of his father.

The doctors at Hines confirmed that Tony did have a lung condition and he was put in the section where he would have bed rest and fresh air. The doctors told us that Tony had probably contracted the disease while he was taking care of soldiers in the hospital in France, especially the ones coming from the prisoner-of-war camps, with all kinds of sicknesses. I was feeling very lost, unhappy and sorry for myself, and wrote to my mum and dad to say I wanted to come home. I received the only letter I ever got from my dad saying, 'you stay put, your husband needs you right now more than we do.' My mum was the letter writer, and her letters kept me going all through the years.

I spent my 18th birthday on the 28th of June in St. Louis. I returned to Chicago, a strange city and strange environment, wondering what was going to happen next. It wasn't all bad, I would go downtown on the streetcar to State street, and look in the shops or go to the Chicago theater to see the shows. On days when the temperature was extremely hot, and the thermometer reached the nineties, we would be sent home early from the factory where I worked. Since there was no air conditioning, we started bringing our bathing suits and towels to work with us. We would walk to North Avenue beach on Lake Michigan and enjoy a cool dip and a lay on the sand. I always had to get back to the house before dark, to keep the peace with Tony's father. He had some very colorful friends from his glory days, when he used to make and sell wine during prohibition.

Those where the violent days. Tony's mum told me that two of her brothers where shot and killed on the street, during the gang wars. His dad did very well; he made enough money to buy a tavern and a restaurant, which allowed them to go on vacation to Sicily for a year. When he came back he had a heart problem, couldn't work anymore, and lost everything. Quite a let down for the family, from Tony's childhood when they had a maid.

One day when I came home from work, there where snails crawling all over the kitchen sink, I had never seen anything like that before. Tony's dad had bought them and was boiling a pot of water to drop them in, he did a lot of the cooking because he was home all day, but I could not eat them. Tony's mum was working part time to help out.

My mum wrote and said things were still rationed in England; there were many food shortages, and I was surrounded by stores with plenty of goods. I decided to send parcels home. I was allowed a 22-pound limit at the post office, so I would get a box together and mail it off about once a month, mostly canned goods, and sugar and assorted goodies. We still didn't have a car so I put the box onto a small wagon and pulled it to the post office. My mum told me years later, that those parcels really helped a lot, it was a few more years before rationing ended, and the country got back to normal.

When Tony's sister Nimfa graduated from grade school she was 14, and his brother Joe was drafted into the army and sent to Korea. His mum was so upset, after just getting her other two sons home from the war. He was gone for two years and came home safely, but his hair turned white. He was only 18 - the same age as me when he left - and almost 20 when he came home.

CHAPTER NINE

In March 1947 I was just leaving the factory for the day, and had planned to take the train out to Maywood to visit Tony when I was met by Tony's sister, Nimfa. She said I had to come home right away, her father had had a heart attack and died. I went straight home and comforted his mother. All of the neighbours where there. She had many friends because she was the only one in the neighbourhood who could read and write Italian and English, and had helped them all answer their letters from Italy. In those days girls where taught to cook and sew and prepare to be married and be a good wife, a higher education was deemed necessary only for the boys.

A huge funeral was planned; the wake lasted three days. There where so many Gardenias, and they where so strong; I could smell them for days afterwards. Tony was brought from the hospital for the day, a long grueling train ride for him, but then he had to go straight back. I was shocked at how big and elaborate everything was; it was a big funeral home and there must have been hundreds of people stopping by. It was so different from the way funerals were in England; they were kept small and private, with only the immediate family attending in the home. If it was in the neighbourhood, all of us children were kept inside and told to be quiet until the funeral procession passed. Tony's mum was worn out, and we were glad when it was over. He was buried at Mt. Carmel cemetery in Chicago; he was 53 years old.

It was March 1957, and now I was free to leave. I told Tony's mum I wanted to find somewhere to live near the hospital in Maywood. I went there and found a room with a family, and got a job within walking distance of the house. I was able to visit more often, and Tony was able to come and visit me since I was closer.

He had been in the hospital a year and a half, and had been given a new experimental drug called streptomycin; it worked on some forms of tuberculosis but not on his. It was then the doctors decided to do surgery on his lung, and that worked. He was discharged in September 1948, two years almost to the day since he went in. I had visited him in the ward with all the other sick guys, and was very lucky that I never caught it; all of the nurses wore masks and I never did. We managed to get a small apartment, and for the first time in three years, lived together on our own in Maywood.

CHAPTER TEN

Our apartment was part of a two-story converted house. The landlady had split the rooms into one-and-a-half units. Because of the housing shortage, we had to share the bathroom with other families. We had a tiny kitchen that was a converted closet. On Friday night she would collect the rent and gamble it away at the Maywood racetrack. She was quite a character; all I remember was that she had a mop of flaming red hair.

I soon found that I was pregnant, and when our landlady found out, she said she wanted two dollars a week more, for using more water with a baby. I told her I would have diaper service, since there was nowhere to wash except the kitchen sink. She said "but you will be rinsing out baby clothes." That's when we all got together and called the O.P.A., which was a government watchdog group, created to stop landlords from gouging people on rent. We were paying sixty dollars a month and when the inspectors came out, they told her to lower the rents, and that she had to build another exit, the house was considered a fire trap.

When I was pregnant, I wrote and told my mum; she wrote back and said, "if you are going to have a family there, you should become an American citizen." We lived across from Proviso high school, so I signed up and took citizenship classes. My instructor, Mrs. Manicure, was from Scotland, so I felt quite at ease. Even though I was married to an American citizen, I still had to go downtown and take the test. I was nervous when the examiner called me in, but I had studied and felt I knew all the answers, even about American history. The first thing he did was put his feet up on the desk and asked, "how are things in the old country?" He was originally from England, and the questions he asked could have been found in the newspaper. Who is the President of the U.S.? Who is the Governor of Illinois? Who declares war? And so on. Needless to say, I got my papers and became a citizen before our first child Bill was born. The instructor did something that would never be tolerated today; he told the group of people waiting for the test and chattering away in all sorts of languages, to go home learn to speak English and then come back for the test.

We bought our first car, an eight-year-old, 1940 Plymouth. New cars still were not being produced, as factories were converting back from war materials to peacetime necessities. We took our first vacation, and drove to Hayward Wisconsin. It was so exciting; after being in America two and a half years I finally got to see some of it. I was about three months pregnant by then. I was still working at the same office, and Tony was going to school under the G.I. bill, a program set up to help all the returning G.I.s finish their education. The doctors had told Tony that he couldn't lift anything heavy, so he took a course in accounting to get an office job. He also worked part time at the post office.

On September 11th 1949, our first son Bill was born. I had always liked the name William, and we put Joseph in the middle for Tony's father. They were not very happy with me, they said it was an Italian tradition to name the first grandchild after the Grandfather, on the father's side. That was the least of our worries. Bill was born with his foot turned outwards. Luckily our wonderful Doctor Green put us in touch with Shriner's Children's hospital and Dr. Schofield, their best surgeon. He operated on him and straightened his foot when he was three weeks old. He went in again at 10 months old and had the heel straightened. It was so hard to leave him there, but the nurses made a fuss over him, they loved to comb his curly hair. I had taken Bill in every two weeks for nine months to have the casts changed on his leg, they thought it would keep his leg growing straight. He learned to walk with the cast on when he was a year old, nothing ever slowed him down.

    We were pretty cramped in that apartment. In that one room, we had a sofa that converted into a bed, a dresser, a kitchen table and chairs, a stove, refrigerator and a crib for Bill, but we managed.

CHAPTER ELEVEN

Tony's brother Joe had come home from Korea in 1949. He bought a 1949 Ford, one of the first ones off the assembly line. They still lived in Chicago, and we all went to see it. We managed to get a bigger apartment in the next suburb, Melrose Park. It had three rooms, a living room, bedroom and kitchen, and Bill was still in a crib in our room.

I was starting to get homesick. I wanted my mum to see Bill, I had sent tons of pictures home, but that wasn't the same. So I got a job across the highway, as a cashier in the cafeteria of a large factory. The hours where five pm until midnight. Tony got home from his job at five o'clock, then I left, and he took care of Bill and put him to bed. I worked there two years, until I saved $800. It cost that for two adult tickets and one child, for a trip on the Queen Mary to England and a trip on the Queen Elizabeth coming back. Tony said we would have to go before he had a regular job.

He was out of school in May, so we booked a trip for a six-month stay; we left in May 1952 and returned in October. Because we were on a ship we were allowed a 500-pound trunk. We filled it up with food, sacks of sugar, canned lunch meat, coffee, tea, even spaghetti and sauce. Food was still rationed in England, and it took them a long time to recover from the war. It was a great trip, Bill talked to everyone on the deck; he was two and a half going on 16. It was smooth sailing and sunny all the way across the Atlantic, until we came close to land, Southampton had a huge dark cloud hanging over it, a sign of things to come. The sun hardly shone the whole summer.

We made our way onto the train to London, and stopped at Kings Cross to get the train to Liverpool. That's where my auntie Lulu met us; it was so great to see her, the first thing Bill did was ask her, "are you my grandma?" He had heard so much about my mum he thought that the first old person he saw would be her. We boarded the train to Liverpool. My sister Margie, her fiancée Gordon and my mum met us at Lime street station with a taxi; I was home after six long years. My mum had my favourite food ready, scouse, which is a Liverpool stew I was raised on. We soon settled in and waited anxiously for the trunk to arrive. It came the next day, leaking sugar; one of the bags had broken, but everything else was intact. We had timed this trip with my sister Margie's wedding; she was being married on my birthday June 28th, 1952. I had borrowed a dress from Tony's cousin, a pretty lime green taffeta, with a headdress. Bill was to be her ring bearer; he had a suit with long pants American style, which fascinated the British people, as all of the English boys wore short pants and knee socks. Margie had a beautiful long white gown, and we both had large bouquets of flowers, it was a great day.

We rented a car and went sightseeing over to Wales to see all the castles. My mum borrowed a stroller and took Bill all over, even on the buses, and she really enjoyed her first Grandchild. Bill had his third birthday over there; we took him to the beach where he road on a donkey; it was fun riding on the ferryboats, across the river Mersey.

That six months went by too fast, before we knew, it was October, and I wanted to stay. I felt we didn't have much to come back to - our furniture was in storage as we had to give up our apartment before we left. We had to come back to continue Bill's treatment at Shriner's Hospital, and Tony said he had to get a job and start work. There wasn't much of a chance for work in England, the country was still recovering from the war and there was still bomb damage in the city. Worst of all was the weather, the sun never shone, and it was cool and cloudy all the time. Tony was used to the sunny American weather, and it seemed there was so much against us. My mum said I was much better off in America. We left my house in a taxi in the pouring rain; it was so hard saying goodbye to my mum. Bill had carried his favourite stuffed animal with him, and when we got on the train it was gone. In all the confusion of leaving he had dropped it in the gutter outside of our house; it had landed in a puddle while getting in the taxi where my mum found it. She dried it out and mailed it to us as we left for America.

I wrote to my mum and told her about Bill's foot. He was now on a built-up shoe, with a one-and-a-half inch sole. He was losing a half an inch a year because it wouldn't grow as fast as the other leg. I didn't want her to be surprised, as I had not told her anything; I didn't want her to worry. She told me later that it took so long for me to get to the point in that letter that she was relieved when I finally did; she thought I was going to tell her something real bad, that he was blind or retarded.

We boarded the train from Liverpool to London, then on to Southampton where we boarded the Queen Elizabeth. It was a much different trip going back; we had very rough seas. Bill and I were so seasick, we had to pass up the dining room, but Tony was fine, he never missed a meal. Even half of the crew was down.

We had 70-mile-an hour winds, and the waves stood straight up. I lay in my bunk watching an apple roll back and forth. We decided to go sit up on the deck and get some fresh air; that helped. That took care of the theory that the two biggest ships in the world would not have a problem in rough seas, they were tossed around like toys. At least we got to sail on the Queen Mary, that made up for missing it the first time, on my way to the states. I was sad after leaving home again, saying goodbye to my mum. That was so hard, especially after she had got to know her grandson, but we had to get back to our life in America.

CHAPTER TWELVE

The ship pulled into New York harbour, and we were standing next to one of the funnels when it blasted off. Bill must have jumped two feet in the air; it was so loud and that funnel so big, you could drive a train through it. It must have really shook him up, because he never forgot it. We then made our way to Grand Central station, to board the train to Chicago. Tony's brother picked us up, and took us to his mum's house; we had to stay with them until we could find a place to live. I went out to Maywood, where we knew some people, actually a French G.I. bride I had met at a G.I. bride club I had attended when I first came over. Her husband was the janitor of a building, and managed to get us a three-room apartment over a store, right around the corner from where we lived when Bill was born.

We moved in just before Christmas, so we were only with his mum for two months, October and November. We got our furniture out of storage, and settled down in Maywood again. That was when we started staying home on Christmas, because Bill didn't want to leave his toys, so the whole family came to visit us on Christmas day, from Chicago. Tony went back to work, and I stayed home with Bill.

We bought a car, as we had sold the other one when we left for England, and I decided it was time to learn to drive. We had a neighbour named Mickie, with three little boys who played with Bill, and she volunteered to take me out to practice. Tony was close enough to his job to walk to the office, so the car was available during the day. That's how I learned to drive, I practiced on the weekends with Tony. I had a hard time with the clutch; there where no automatic cars in those days, and everything had a shift. I was very happy when automatic drive came out a few years later, before we bought our next car.

While we were living in Maywood, my aunt Norah came to visit us, it was so good to have somebody from home. She was not really related, but a life-long friend of my mum. Norah had belonged to the Salvation Army all of her adult life, and had been transferred to America; she was living in the retired officer's residence in Asbury Park, New Jersey. Norah and my mum were good friends since they were children. My mum was from a big family, and Norah was an only child; my Grandma included her in the family, as she wasn't treated very well at home. When she was fourteen she was put into service; in England that meant working for a rich family as a scullery maid, cleaning, scrubbing floors, etc.

The following year, I found I was pregnant. Bill was four years old and was very excited; he wanted a baby brother. He got his wish on May 4th, 1954; his baby brother Jim was born. Bill was so thrilled; he put his precious baseball and bat in the crib, we told him, "you're going to have to wait a while before he can play with you." Jim was born in Westlake hospital in Melrose Park, the same place Bill was born in, and by the same doctor Green, who helped us with Bill.

It was starting to get a little crowded in the apartment now, so we looked around for a bigger place, and found one ten minutes away in Melrose Park. It had five rooms on the first floor; the landlord lived upstairs, and it had a nice-sized yard to play in. Bill turned five that year in September, and started kindergarten at the local Catholic school. It was only a few blocks away, so I put Jim in the stroller and walked Bill over there, dropped him off after saying hello to the nun, and walked back to the apartment. As soon as we arrived I heard a voice behind me saying "hi, mum." Bill had followed us home. He said, "that was fun." He thought he was now through with school. He said, "but I went!" I had to take him back, and eventually he did settle in. I think it was just that I had a new baby now, and he thought he was being replaced. Little did he realize, he had 20 years of school ahead of him. We bought a car about that time, a two-tone blue Oldsmobile, used but in good condition. We also had Jim christened, Tony's brother Joe, and his wife Val were GodParents.

Surprise, surprise: when Jim was only five months old, I found I was pregnant again. I didn't expect that, it had taken so long to have the second one. Our number three son, Randy, was born on July 26th, 1955. I kidded doctor Green that he didn't know how to deliver girls, and he said, "don't complain, I can't even get one, I have three boys."

Our landlord was not happy. He had been leery about renting to people with children, but since I only had one, and a small baby, he had said O.K. His wife was ill, and he wanted us to be quiet all the time; that was hard to do with two babies. We had become friendly with a real nice couple, Barbara and Ernie Piche, who had three small children. We left all the kids with Ernie and Tony while we went to a movie for a much needed break. Half way through the movie, I started having labour pains while I was driving; Barb couldn't drive. Luckily we only lived three blocks from Westlake Hospital, where Bill and Jim were born. I drove past it on the way to the house, and dropped her off so she could watch the kids with Ernie while I picked up Tony. I just made it, doctor Green was washing his hands when Randy was born, the only one I was fully awake for. I got the name Randy from doctor Green, he had a son named Randy, that he talked about all the time.

Tony told me that Jim, who was only 14 months old, didn't understand why I had suddenly disappeared overnight. He walked around the house, looking in closets saying, "mummie," when I came home after four days, he didn't want anything to do with me. It was as if he was saying, "you have a new baby now, you don't need me." Tony had to help him in and out of the high chair, and change and feed him. It was especially hard since I was breast-feeding Randy, and there was Bill to look after. We went out and bought Jim a rocking horse, but he wouldn't look at it - figured it was a bribe - as if to say, "you have a new toy, so now you have given me one." He waited until Randy was big enough to get on it, then they fought over it constantly, and they both wanted to ride it at the same time. Our landlady was not well and kept asking us to be quiet, but that was hard with a one-year old and a two-year old, so we decided its time to move, again.

First we had Randy christened at the same church were Bill went to kindergarten. This time we had Tony's younger brother Lou for the Godfather, and my friend Eunice from England as Godmother.

CHAPTER THIRTEEN

Hoffman Estates is a town that grew up in the farmland and cornfields near an area called Schaumburg, about thirty miles west of Chicago. The town was built by F&S construction, a father and son company from Arizona. It was one of many subdivisions built around the country out of necessity, since their was a big housing shortage in the 1950s. This was a lifesaver for families like us; it was only $800 down for ex G.I.s. Before that, the standard rule for a down payment was one-third the price of the house. That put houses out of reach to most young people. Tony's brother Santo had bought one for his mother in another subdivision called Rolling Meadows in 1955, so we looked in the same area.

We left Bill and the two babies with Tony's mum while we went to check out the models we saw advertised in the paper. The original section of the town was already built up in 1955; when we went looking in 1956, the second phase was planned and there were only three models built for us to look at. They were sitting in a field on Higgins Road when we first saw them. It was in the middle of a snowstorm in February. They had a huge map on the wall, showing how the town would look when it was built. We picked out a street and stuck a thumbtack on the house we would like, and that is how we bought our first and only house.

To qualify, we had to make $100 a week; that was the monthly mortgage payment; after we put the $800 down, we went back to Tony's mum to pick up the kids. We were really shaking, to think we had just signed our lives away for the next 25 years. Santo poured us a drink to celebrate, then all we had to do was wait and see if it went through. We went out every weekend, to see how the houses were going up. We got the O.K. that we had qualified, but it was July before we heard that we could move in; the house was ready. We were so excited, it had been 10 years since I had come to America, and we had made many moves from apartment to apartment. Our Bill was 7 years old, Jim was 2, and Randy had his first Birthday on July 26th after we moved in. It was the best thing we ever did; all of our neighbours were around the same age, with little kids, and most were ex-G.I.s.

It was a great place for them to grow up; they all had someone to play with. It was safe and quiet, with a dead-end street and a cornfield two doors away, and nothing in the distance but Schaumburg Church, a beautiful old church dating back to the Civil War. There was one big farm left, and the owner refused to sell the land. He still had cows, we could hear them mooing in the morning. We had great neighbours, and some good get-togethers; block parties and a card club. Almost everyone had four or five children; one family had seven. Since no one had much money, we entertained ourselves. We couldn't afford baby sitters, so we formed a babysitter club and sat for each other; for hours instead of money.

We were allowed a maximum of 15 hours, then we had to pay it back. It was a pretty good system, born out of necessity; the oldest children in the neighbourhood were Bill and Johnny Kocher, age seven and eight, and the Allen boys. Diane and Fran lived next door, and Sally and Jack across the street. No one had families around, and of course, and I had no one here. It was like a family, we were all around the same age, and excited to be in our first home. I was the only one in the neighbourhood who could drive; they had all moved from Chicago and had been able to walk everywhere or ride buses. So it fell to me to teach them to drive, mostly to sit next to them when they needed to practice. Luckily there wasn't much traffic in those days, the streets were pretty quiet. I only drove to Rolling Meadows once a week to take Grandma Provenzano shopping for groceries; we only had one car, so Tony would get a ride one day a week. There was no transportation; the closest train was five miles away in Roselle, so the car was an absolute necessity.

We were in the house less than a year when I found I was pregnant again, on October 29th, 1957 our one and only girl was born. We were all thrilled, especially Tony's mum, and we named our daughter after her, Grace Marie. It sounded much nicer in Italian, Gratzie Maria. I made the name stay together, because I didn't want her to be called Gracie. We had her christened, and this time we had Santo and Nimfa for Godparents. I was in the hospital over Halloween, and felt bad leaving those two little ones. Jim was three and Randy was two. I had promised to take them Trick or Treating, when I called home they didn't want to talk, they were too busy counting their candy; Tony and Bill had taken them out, so much for missing mummie, I felt worse than they did.

We did have one terrible tragedy happen that year. My friend Barbara Piche would lend me her bassinet; we took turns and shared it between babies. Just as I got through she would use it; it was a one-year size that we would use for six months, then they went into the crib. Barbara was pregnant with her fourth baby, against the advice of her doctor. She had already had three cesarean births, and that was supposed to be the limit. I was waiting for her to pick up the bassinet after the baby was born. I called the hospital to ask how she was doing, as we were all worried, and was told she had died. The doctors tried for hours to save her, but she bled to death. The baby lived and Ernie had four children to raise without a mother; he had no luck with baby sitters and finally re-married. We lost track of him after that, after he picked up the bassinet, so sad.

We settled into our new home. We put in a sandbox and swing set for the kids. Our yard was like the neighbourhood playground, but I didn't mind; it kept them safe and I knew where they were. I made gallons of Kool-Aid for them in the Summer. Bill started school across the highway, Higgins Road, and some of the mothers and I had to form a patrol to get them over safely. It was only a two-lane highway in 1956. By the second year, the new school on our side was built, then he had a short walk, up the hill.

We had a parent teacher meeting to name the school, and we voted to name it Fairview. Bill played on a little league baseball team at the school playground, and Tony was a Coach and Manager. We had some good times, with all the kids in the league. It was a great place to raise kids; quiet, safe streets, and we never worried about locking doors or bringing toys inside, no one bothered anything. There were only three houses on our side of the street with the cornfield at the end, so I didn't have to worry about traffic.

Schaumburg's main street consisted of three taverns and an Ace hardware store. We went to Rolling Meadows for shopping, and Palatine for church. The priest, Father Sullivan, decided to bring the church to us, so Tony and Bill and some other men set up folding chairs, threw a sheet over the bar in the Buggy Whip lounge on Roselle Road, and we had Mass there. When someone complained about kneeling on the hardwood floor, we told them, "If Father Sullivan can do it, you can." He called it "Old St. Buggy Whip." That was our church until St. Hubert's was built two years later. Tony was an usher, and helped to raise money to build the church.

CHAPTER FOURTEEN

We had been in our new house two-and-a-half years, then in 1959, I found out I was pregnant again. On August 28th, our fourth son Steven was born. I wanted to name him Anthony after his Dad, but Tony said no, he didn't want him to end up being called junior, so we put Anthony in the middle.

Bill was almost ten years old now; he was losing a half-inch a year on his leg, and was now walking on a built-up shoe, with a five-inch sole. The doctors at Shriner's said they could do a bone lengthening operation and give him the five inches back. That summer, we took him out of his little league baseball team, and had him admitted into Shriner's. We were waiting for the operation, when the surgeons told us that even if they got him the inches back, he would lose five more over the next ten years, because he was still growing and would probably reach his full height by age 20, and the lengthening procedure could only be done once.

His Dad had to give permission for the leg to be amputated at the shin, then he could be fitted with an artificial leg and wear regular shoes. We all went to the hospital and held Steven up to the window so he could see him, children were not allowed in the hospitals in those days, in case they carried diseases. Bill came home in October and the new artificial limb was fitted. He amazed everyone at how well he adapted to it. He was out riding his bike, nothing ever slowed him down. The local Herald newspaper sent a reporter to the house to do a story on him and take a family picture, we still have that photo.

The following summer he was right back playing baseball, and a few years later, in high school, he even played football. The doctors always said he should be able to walk normally because he had his knee intact and the artificial limb was below the knee and he shouldn't limp. Shriner's took care of him until he was 16 and kept the artificial limb repaired; they didn't mind because that meant he was active.

Bill was in school and the four younger ones were home all day. Steven was one, Grace Marie was three, Randy was four, and Jim was five. We sometimes wished we could stretch the house, it was a tight squeeze with seven of us. We were constantly switching rooms, first we had the biggest bedroom, then we turned it into a bunkhouse for the boys with a single bed for Bill and bunk beds for Jim and Randy. We had Grace Marie and Steven in the small bedroom and we were in the middle room. Then we decided she needed privacy being the only girl, so we gave her the small bedroom. She still went into the boy's room and climbed up into the bunk bed. Four of them under five were quite a handful. One time Jim and Randy got into a can of house paint that had been left on the picnic table, and they painted each other. I had to throw their clothes and shoes out.

I needed to do something to help out with the bills. I did not want to leave them all with a baby sitter, so I took in two boys; Jerry was a one-year-old, and his brother

Donny Lee was three years old. It was like kindergarten here; they played together, we made cookies, and I made Play Dough out of flour, water and food coloring; we had a great time. We had the swingset and sandbox, and a small pool in the yard to keep them busy.

We had a dog we had bought for Bill named Corkie; he was a blonde Cocker mix. Corkie was a good little dog, he had to be, with those boys picking on him. Over the year that followed, I watched up to eight neighbourhood kids for lunch, including Gail Kocher from next door, Grace Marie's friend, and another neighbourhood boy, Kelly Stroud.

When they all finally went to school, I was able to get a part-time job. The neighbours and I drove together to Elk Grove Village, about six miles away and I worked for Ampex recording company, boxing cassette tapes. It was just during school hours, so I never did leave them with a baby sitter, I got home at 3:30 every day, just as they got home from school.

CHAPTER FIFTEEN

During all this time, I wanted my mum to see the children. There was no way we could afford for all of us to go to England, so she made the trip over here in 1963, for one month. It was great, but the month went by too fast.

Before she came, we bought our first new car, a 1963 Pontiac Station Wagon. We had been pushing our old car as far as we could, and knew we'd never be able to take her anywhere if we get a new car. It was perfect for all of us, a nine-passenger capacity. As the kids grew up, we all piled in and went camping around Illinois and Wisconsin. We packed the tent on the roof; they kids screamed when it blew off on the highway; we drove back and picked it up. All the kids got new bikes that year.

It was really hard to say goodbye to my mum. I sat on the picnic table and cried after she left; she was a dear little mum, and I missed her great sense of humour. She made everyone laugh with her typical Liverpool humour. I once asked her how she could get up in the morning and be in such a good mood and she said, "When I look at our Billy who can't see, what have I got to complain about?" I try to keep that in mind when I feel cranky.

Two months later my sister Margie, her husband Gordon and their twins boys Gary and Stephen decided to come over for a visit. I was glad we had the station wagon then, as there were now eleven of us to get in the car. It was hot and sunny that July and they loved it; it had been raining steadily in England for weeks before they left. They all started out wearing their heavy British clothes, and by the time they went home they were in shorts. We had some great days out at the lakes, and have movies taken at Devil's lake in Wisconsin. The boys loved uncle Tony's Pontiac, when they would all start acting up in the back, Tony would say "I'm going to press the ejector button and you will all shoot out of the back," they would then sit quietly for a while, then realize he was only kidding.

We were surprised how much further ahead the twins were; they had already been in school two years, and could read very well. Grace Marie was four months younger and had only been in kindergarten; they were six in June and she was six in October. I couldn't tell them apart, I would sit them down and say, "You're Gary and you're Stephen?" They would say, "lets mix ourselves up," run around in a circle, and then ask, "who are we now?" Gordon called our Steve "Jet," because he was always running. Gordon walked them all over, and said, "I am starting an American children's walking club, he wasn't used to seeing kids being driven everywhere. There was no transportation out here, so we relied heavily on the car. None of these subdivisions could have existed without the car, all the men had to drive to work, and we didn't have buses close by like they did in England.

It was a pretty insulated world, revolving around school, sports and family. We got together with the neighbours for block parties and cards; it was good for all of us mothers, being all around the same age, and the children always had someone to play with.

When the kids were old enough to go camping, all seven of us climbed into the station wagon, complete with luggage rack and sliding window in the back door. We tied a Sears nine-person canvas tent to the roof along with sleeping bags, gas Coleman stove and lantern, a cooler full of food and took off. We started out locally at Rock Cut and Starved Rock State Parks in Illinois, stopped at Gettysburg Pennsylvania, and eventually made it to Indiana Dunes and Warren Dunes in Michigan.

In 1964, we camped in Pennsylvania and New Jersey, and ended up at the New York World's Fair in Flushing. Steve still remembers the giant US ROYAL TIRE that was actually a Ferris Wheel.

We camped in upstate New York, drove to the Bronx, and took the subway to Battery Park to see the Statue of Liberty. When we boarded the subway back, the doors closed quickly and everyone except Billy made it on the train. We took off and watched him disappear on the platform. Luckily, he boarded the next train and we all met up at the end of the line – we could have lost him forever.

After my mum left, I decided to try and join a British club; I thought I would feel better with someone from home to talk to. The first one I tried was a group called "The Daughters of the British Empire," but that was hopeless; they marched around with the Union Jack flag and were so serious. I don't think any of them had ever set foot in England. The next one was at someone's house, and not very friendly, I said one more try and the third time was lucky. It was called the T.B.P.A. Transatlantic Bride's and Parent's Association, formed in England, so parents could charter a plane to visit children here, and G.I. brides could charter planes to go home. I joined the club and was delighted to meet three women from the Liverpool area. There was lots of talking and cups of tea; I really enjoyed it. We had Christmas parties and picnics, and great get-togethers with other families. They had some low-priced tickets for members to go to England; I decided right then to go to work and save enough money for the whole family to go over, so they could see were I came from.

That was in 1964. It took me five years to save up enough, but we made it in 1969; I took the four younger ones home for two months, then Tony followed with Bill for the second month. Tony only had three week's vacation coming and took one without pay, and Bill was working and saving for college. Jim and Randy objected at first because we had to take them out of little league, and Grace Marie didn't want to leave her friend Gail next door. They were all happy and excited to go on their first plane ride, and once we got to England they had a great time.

It was a whole different life in England. Here they had to be driven everywhere and over there they could ride on the double-decker buses, go down to the pier on the river Mersey, ride the ferry boat across, run along the sand beach, and go to the fun fair, carnival and rides, with penny slot machines they could play. Gambling was already legal in England, so they got a kick out of that. They made many friends in the neighborhood, and taught the local boys how to play baseball, out in a nearby soccer field. When Tony and Bill came over we rented a car and drove to Wales, through the Mersey tunnel, so they could see all the castles. We stayed overnight in a bed & breakfast cottage, and it was a great trip.

It was a bit crowded at my mum's little house. I had Grace Marie in with me, and the boys had my brother Billy's room; when Bill and Tony came over it was even more crowded, then Bill's girlfriend Jean decided to come too. Luckily the mother of our boys' new friends, Margaret Jones, invited Steve, Bill and Jean to stay with their boys and girls. She was wonderful, and we still keep in touch to this day. I don't know how my mum kept up with us all, cooking for so many of us every day. Grace Marie made friends too, with the daughters of my old friend Dolly Jones; Steve was friends with Frankie Jones, and Jim had Davy Jones following him around everywhere. Bill got along great with their Dad, Frank, who took him to the pub for a pint. Bill was 19, and couldn't go in a pub in America, so he felt like a grown-up there.

We had one great party, and my brother Bobby sang for us. He had a great voice, and quite a following in the local pubs. My dad did his party-piece too, and my auntie Doris sang; she had a beautiful voice as well. Those two months went by so fast; we bid my mum and family a tearful goodbye, and drove off toward London. We stopped along the way to see Warwick Castle and some of the lovely countryside, and ended up in London at a bed & breakfast place for the night.

We had one day left to see London before we had to board the plane at Heathrow airport. I was determined that they were going to see as much as possible, in case they never got back over there again, so we got up early and headed for the city. They fed the pigeons in Trafalgar Square, Steve sat on all the lions at Nelson's Column, and we toured the houses of Parliament and all the sights, and ended up on a boat trip on the Thames, to the Tower of London. We toured the Tower and saw the crown jewels, and the block where some of Henry the Eighth's queens were beheaded. I wouldn't even let them stop to eat, since we had only allowed one day to see as much as possible. I did break down and let them have an ice cream.

We got back to our hotel exhausted, managed to find a fish and chip shop still open and finally had some supper. I am so glad we did it, it was the only trip we made over there together, then it was on the plane and back home the next day. We got the six-hour time difference back; we left London in the afternoon, and were walking around our back garden the same afternoon, amazing.

It was a trip to remember; Bill married his girlfriend Jean and a year later, they went back to England on their honeymoon. Grace Marie made it back once with her girl friend, and Steve went back with us twice over the years; but Jim and Randy never did go again.

In 1970 we camped at Illinois Beach State Park, Indiana Dunes and Warren dunes, camping all around Lake Michigan. We parked the camper and visited Mackinac Island; still no cars allowed there. One night, Randy was filling the camp stove with fuel and it spilled on his bare feet. One of them caught fire – he jumped around until it went out. Luckily, only the fuel burned, and he did not.

That night, all the kids put their wet PF Flyers around the camp fire to dry out, and we all went to bed. The next morning, they had melted into blobs of canvas and rubber.

In 1972, Tony and I took Steve and Grace camping for their first trip to Disney World and Fort Wilderness Campground. Steve enjoyed it, but Grace wasn't so thrilled.

Eventually, we settled into a routine - the kids in school and Bill in college. I was very homesick and had a hard time settling; we even discussed going back there to live, but we would have to sell our house to do it, and that was too big of a risk with five children to think about. We then decided to go back for a visit as often as possible, and managed to make the trip every other year in the seventies. I was able to work part-time and save up for tickets.

The only time I flew home alone was in 1976 when my Dad died. I went home to be with my mum; it was in February, in the damp cold, miserable English weather. My mum had the gas fire going in the bedroom, she was afraid I would get sick, not being used to being without central heat anymore. When I got home, I worried about my Mum, so Tony and I went back in August for a visit.

CHAPTER SIXTEEN

My sister Margie and I decided that my brother Billy would come over here or go to Australia and live near one of us, with my Mum; in case anything happened to her, Billy would have some one to care for him. My brother Bobby's wife, Maureen, wanted no part of it, so we both tried to get them out of England. It was very traumatic for my mum; she had lived in our house in Fazakerley for 50 years, but she wanted to see Bill settled. She visited me for six weeks and Margie for six weeks, and decided on Australia. They had good benefits for him and my mum, plus great weather, so they could be outdoors.

My mum said it would be too much for me, having five children to care for, so we went over and saw her off to Australia in 1978. She had nine good years there and died in 1987, two weeks before her 80th Birthday. Meanwhile our Bill had made it all the way through college and on to Law school; after graduation, he passed the bar the first time, and we were so proud of him. He took off for Europe with Jean for a well-deserved vacation; they had a great time sightseeing, and finally ended up at my mum's in Fazakerley for a visit before heading home.

In 1979, the year after my mum came for a visit, we had the worst year ever. First Tony went in the hospital for triple bypass heart surgery in April, and we all visited him on mother's day in May. He was home for eight-weeks recuperating, and ready to go back to work after the July Fourth holiday. We had a family picnic in the yard, and didn't know that was the last time we would all be together as a complete family.

It was a gorgeous sunny day; the next night on July 5th, Randy was killed on his motorcycle. He only had the bike for a couple of months. I had begged him not to buy it, as I had done with Jim, who had his for a year. I told them I didn't want any of them to get a motorcycle, since my uncle Bill had been killed on his in England. Once they moved out they got one anyway. Randy was hit by a woman in a car, pulling out of a restaurant not one mile from home; she said she never saw him, and that he had his headlight on. We had gone to bed early that night, and didn't hear the sirens.

Grace Marie saw the accident and followed the ambulance to the hospital; the paramedics came out of the emergency room and gave her the bike keys and said, "he's gone." It was after midnight, and she went to the phone and called her brothers. They sat in Jim's apartment all night, afraid to come and wake their Dad in case the shock would be too much, as he was still recuperating. They finally all came here at seven o'clock in the morning and woke Tony first. He woke me and when I saw his white face I thought he was having a relapse. Then I walked into the family room and saw Father Brennan, our priest. I knew it was bad, the whole family was there.

The rest of the day was just a blur, we were all numb with shock, to think such a lovable, handsome, healthy son was gone from us, forever. He was buried at St. Michael's Cemetery near us, across from Harper College, where he had gone to school.

He wanted to be a Carpenter; both he and Jim liked working with their hands and being outdoors.

His death was listed as July 6th, because it was after midnight of the 5th, when he reached the hospital. The next day was a constant stream of people coming and going, everyone was in shock. The family, the neighbours and all of his many friends were here. There were so many people at the funeral home, and so many cars following him to cemetery; it was so sad, and on another beautiful sunny Summer day.

It was the kind of day Randy would have been out golfing, swimming, or playing ball with his buddies. He was good at everything he tried, very athletic. We bought two lots next to him and that is where his Dad and I are going to be, we didn't want him to be alone. It will be 33 years in three months, on July 6th 2012 when he would have been 57. I just can't picture him 57, he will always be 23 to us.

CHAPTER SEVENTEEN

It was a very hard year to get through, we all missed Randy so much. He was the one who got along with everyone. By the end of the Summer the house got too quiet. Jim had already moved into his own apartment, Grace Marie had recently moved out, and Bill was married and gone. Steve was the only one still at home, and he went away to college in September. So there we were, back to the two of us. After years of phones ringing and the screen door banging, and "Hi, Mum I'm home," it was so hard to get used to.

Life goes on, I had to pull myself together for the sake of the others, and Tony. As Grace Marie said, "you still have us Mum.," That snapped me out of my self-pity; and we still had Tony, their dad to worry about. He was still trying to cope and get stronger every day. He finally did go back to work, and we all tried to get back into the routine of living. Steve had saved up to buy a motorcycle, so the three brothers could ride together, after the accident he bought a guitar with the money. I had to get back to my Trim Club classes; I had been teaching classes on nutrition for weight reduction. I couldn't cry all the time and stand in front of the class with swollen eyes, so it helped me pull myself together.

In 1981 we had some wonderful news; Bill and Jean told us they were expecting a baby. We were so thrilled about having our first grandchild. Then on July 23rd, 1982, Adam was born. They were going to call him Randy, but decided on Adam with Randy as a middle name. As Bill said, we couldn't replace Randy, and Adam had to be his own person. We thought we would never become grandparents, Bill and Jean were married for 12 years before they had him. They both wanted to finish school first, and they did. That really started something. Grace Marie decided to get married that year in November, to Ed. We had a big wedding in a great place called the Barn of Barrington. It was a happy time, but a worrisome time for me. I had found out through a routine physical that I had a tumor about the size of a grapefruit in my middle. I didn't tell anyone but Tony, as not to miss or spoil the wedding. I waited until after Thanksgiving as Jim was here from Florida. I was admitted in December and the tumor had doubled from five to ten pounds. It was removed, and it turned out to be an ovarian cyst; thank God it wasn't cancerous. After that good news we had a good Christmas.

The following year, in April, Jim decided to get married in Florida to a girl named Billie Jo, (B.J.). We all flew there for the wedding; it was in the Ocala Forest, a beautiful setting, and a gorgeous day. It had rained the day before and it stormed the day after, we really lucked out. The whole family went and since there were so many of us, with Adam in the car seat, we rented a big, black Lincoln Town car. I can only imagine what the bride's family thought when we drove into the woods in it, probably "here comes the mob from Chicago."

It was beautiful; B.J. already had a little girl named Lynn, three years old, whom Jim ended up raising as his own. She was the Flower Girl, and very pretty. Tony and I went back one year later in April for the birth of his daughter, Andrea, our second Grand child. The following year in February, 1985, Grace Marie had her first baby, a boy named Erick. He was a big baby, 10 pounds, and she had a real hard time, ending up with a cesarean birth. Adam had also weighed 10 pounds.

In 1986, Bill and Jean had their second baby, a girl. They named her Amanda, and she weighed almost eight-and-a-half pounds. In February 1987, Grace Marie had her second baby, a girl, and named her Lauren. She and her husband Bobby now have a son, Jaden, who's almost three. In 1988, Jim had his second baby, a girl, and they named her Heather. Now we had six grandchildren, and I had thought we wouldn't have any. They were all beautiful babies, and I was so pleased that they all had such nice names, some of the names they come up with these days are dreadful, I can't even pronounce them, I think they make them up.

CHAPTER EIGHTEEN

All of the Grand children are grown up now, and we have six Great Grand children. Our first Grand child, Adam, has Sierra now 12 years old, Dylan eight years old, and Marley, six years old. Our second Grand child Andrea has a girl named Emma, almost seven, and a son named Jonathan, almost three. Erick our third Grand child has a boy named Jason, nine years old and a girl named Jocelyn, who's almost seven. That brings the family up to today.

Tony and I are enjoying our retirement years; he has been retired 26 years now. We have enjoyed traveling, and have seen much of the world. Australia twice, England many times, all over Europe, and all over the States while attending his army reunions, held every two years in different states. We've also been to Hawaii and Canada. On our last visit to England we traveled through Ireland, Wales and Scotland. We are very blessed to have lived this long, especially with all the operations we've had. Tony at least 12, myself 4, and we've lived long enough to see all of our children grow up and see them have children. Now we're on to the next generation, with seven great Grandchildren.

I realize that I have skipped many details, but this Biography will fill in some of the blanks for that next generation, and to let you all know that Dad and I
LOVE YOU ALL LOTS! Mum.

To Our Mum

What more can a mother do, but give her life to her children?
She left her English home, to cross the sea and start a new life.
To give all her heart, and soul, and time, and energy.
To teach, and hold, and inspire, and love her children with all she has,
in every way possible.

To live and love by selfless, humble example and sacrifice.
To lift her children and their wonderful father up before herself.
To surround herself with joy and peace, and timeless affection.
To show her endless forgiveness for our words spoken out of hand.
To build a house of warmth and comfort; of Christmas Dinners, and Thanksgiving cheer,
and a welcoming peace.

You are always there for us.

We could never ask for more, and all we can do is make sure you know:
We love you and dad with all our hearts.

    Your Son,

    Steven

    January 26, 2009

Made in the USA
Lexington, KY
07 February 2019